Naked Gardening

The Natural, Bare Rooted Way To Cultivate Your Garden and Your Soul While Nude

Kristin Williams

© 2024

Copyright © 2024

All rights reserved. No part of this book may be reproduced in any form without permission in writing from the author. Reviewers may quote brief passages in reviews.

Disclaimer

No part of this publication may be reproduced or transmitted in any form or by any means, mechanical or electronic, including photocopying or recording, or by any information storage and retrieval system, or transmitted by email without permission in writing from the publisher.

While all attempts and efforts have been made to verify the information held within this publication, neither the author nor the publisher assumes any responsibility for errors, omissions, or opposing interpretations of the content herein.

This book is for entertainment purposes only. The views expressed are those of the author alone, and should not be taken as expert instruction or commands. The reader of this book is responsible for his or her own actions when it comes to reading the book.

Adherence to all applicable laws and regulations, including international, federal, state, and local governing professional licensing, business practices, advertising, and all other aspects of doing business in the US, Canada, or any other jurisdiction is the sole responsibility of the purchaser or reader.

Neither the author nor the publisher assumes any responsibility or liability whatsoever on the behalf of the purchaser or reader of these materials. Any received slight of any individual or organization is purely unintentional.

Introduction

Hello fellow earth lovers and bare enthusiasts! I'm Kristin, your guide to a world where garden gloves might be optional, but clothes are definitely not on the guest list.

My journey into naked gardening started quite by accident, or perhaps it was fate, dressed up as a particularly hot summer day. There I was, sweat clinging onto every fiber of my T-shirt, the sun beating down mercilessly. Looking around, ensuring no nosy neighbors were in sight, I thought, "Why not?" Off went the clothes, and what started as a desperate attempt to cool down became my gardening revelation. Feeling the breeze on my skin and the sun warming every part of me equally was liberating! The tomatoes didn't seem to mind, and the carrots, let's just say, seemed perkier.

Since that fateful day, my garden has seen more of me than most spas have. And why not? Gardening naked isn't just about avoiding tan lines or laundry (though those are definite perks). It's about reconnecting with nature in the most literal sense. Every leaf brushed against my skin, every mud-squish between toes, became a sensory celebration. Trust me, there's nothing quite like chasing a runaway zucchini across the yard with nothing on—it's invigorating and a fantastic way to ensure your veggies respect you.

But let's address the overgrown elephant in the room—yes, gardening nude does come with its own set of challenges. There's the occasional bee who mistakes you for a particularly large and attractive flower, and let's not start on the neighbors' cat who seems to have developed a rather pointed interest in my herbaceous borders. And of course, safety first: one must remember where the thorny roses are planted, and hot tea should be handled with care (and perhaps a strategically placed apron).

This book isn't just a how-to on planting seeds and pulling weeds sans apparel. It's an invitation to chuckle at the absurdity of it all and to embrace a lifestyle that tickles your fancy—and perhaps other parts too, should you choose to frolic through the ferns. From practical tips on how to keep your privates happy and healthy while hoeing, to heartfelt stories of personal growth and community, I invite you to join me in this journey of discovery.

So, grab your sunscreen, maybe a hat for the more sensitive areas, and let's get to the root of naked gardening together. Whether you're a seasoned nudist or just a curious newbie, there's room in this garden for all. After all, beneath our clothes, we're all just gardeners, trying to make the world a little greener and our spirits a little lighter.

Let's make every day a bit more of a natural wonder!

Preparing to Plant Bare

Ah, the great outdoors! There's nothing quite like the feeling of soil slipping through your fingers, especially when the rest of you is as free as the day you were born. Welcome to the foundational chapter of our naked gardening adventure, where we'll strip down the basics of preparing to plant—bare and unbridled.

First things first, let's talk about the elephant in the garden—yes, gardening in your birthday suit does require a bit of forethought, unless you fancy explaining to a confused mail carrier why you're mulching in the nude. But fear not! I'm here to guide you through setting up your personal Eden where you can prune, plant, and pluck to your heart's content, sans wardrobe.

Over the years, I've learned (sometimes the hard way) that a successful naked gardener isn't just about embracing nature in the buff; it's also about planning. It's about knowing when the sun is just right, where the nosy neighbors can't see, and most importantly, which plants are less likely to send you running for an ice pack. Yes, I'm looking at you, stinging nettles.

In this chapter, I'll share the secrets of timing your gardening sessions to avoid those awkward sunburns (and the even more awkward explanations to your dermatologist). We'll choose the perfect spot in your garden where privacy meets sunlight, and you can sunbathe as much as you sun-care for your plants. Plus, I'll give you the scoop on the tools that make gardening naked not just a joy, but a breeze—literally and figuratively.

So, shed your inhibitions (and your clothes, if you haven't already), grab a hat (for your head, of course), and let's prepare to plant with nothing but nature as our companion. Whether you're a seasoned nudist or just looking to add a little zest to your horticultural pursuits, this chapter will make sure you're well-equipped to tackle your gardening goals—while tackling the unique challenges of doing it au naturel. Let's get started, shall we? After all, there's no better way to connect with Mother Earth than connecting with her as Mother Nature intended!

Choosing the Right Time For Naked Gardening

Timing is everything, especially when your garden attire consists of nothing but the sky above and the earth below. Choosing the right time for naked gardening is a bit like selecting the perfect moment to skinny-dip in your backyard pond—timing must be impeccable to ensure maximum enjoyment and minimal surprises.

Let's delve into understanding the best conditions for baring it all in the garden. The sun, that glorious beacon of warmth, deserves our first nod. Basking in the morning sun or enjoying the last rays of the day can be pure bliss. These golden hours—early morning or late afternoon—are not just beautiful, they're kinder to your skin too, shielding you from the harsh midday rays that could turn your naked escapade into a less-than-pleasant experience.

Now, consider the weather. Clear, calm days are your best bet. You don't want to be caught in a gusty wind that sends you sprinting for cover, or worse, a surprise shower. Keeping an eye on the weather forecast can be as crucial as any other preparation in your gardening schedule.

Privacy, oh sweet privacy! It's paramount unless you plan on becoming the talk of the town. Align your gardening times with those quiet moments when neighbors are less likely to be around. Early mornings when the world is still waking up, or midday during work hours, can be ideal. Take a look around your garden, note where you might be visible to neighbors, and plan accordingly.

Seasons change and so does the suitability of gardening in the nude. Spring and summer are glorious with their warm soil and gentle breezes, inviting you to spend hours amidst nature's bounty. Fall, while cooler, offers a crispness that can be quite invigorating, just keep something warm at hand for when the chill sets in. Winter might require you to trade nudity for some warmth, unless you're in a climate that laughs at the mention of frost.

Finally, tune into your personal rhythm. Are you an early riser, finding joy in the fresh dawn air? Or does twilight inspire a tranquil mood perfect for gardening? The best time for you will sync with your natural inclinations and the rhythms of your garden life.

So, as we prepare to move on to the next topics, remember that finding the perfect time for naked gardening is about blending environmental savvy with personal comfort and practical privacy. It's about making those moments in the garden as naturally delightful as possible.

Gardening Tools and How To Use Them Safely While Nude

When gardening in the nude, the usual tools—shovels, hoes, pruners—take on an extra layer of intrigue. The freedom of gardening without clothes is thrilling, but it requires a bit of strategic planning when it comes to handling your equipment. Here are some tips to make sure your gardening tools are as safe as they are necessary, without anything extra (like clothes) between you and nature.

Choose the Right Tools: Opt for tools with longer handles to provide a comfortable distance between your bare skin and the soil. This isn't just about comfort—it's about safety. Long-handled tools minimize the risk of accidental scrapes or pokes and allow you to work with a bit more leverage and control, which is always a bonus when you're as free as the breeze.

Mind the Edges: Sharp tools like pruners, shears, or any cutting implements should be handled with extra care. When you're wearing clothes, a small slip might just ruin a garment, but when you're nude, it can ruin your day. Make sure the blades are always sharp (ironically, a sharper tool is safer because it requires less force to use) and store them safely when not in use, ideally in a tool belt or a nearby toolbox.

Protection Where It Counts: Even in the nude, some accessories remain crucial. Gloves are a must. They protect your hands from thorns, splinters, and blisters. Footwear is equally important—sturdy shoes or boots can save your toes from the misfortune of meeting a dropped tool or an unseen rock.

Sunscreen as Your Shield: While not a tool in the traditional sense, sunscreen is an essential ally in the naked gardener's arsenal. Apply a broad-spectrum sunscreen generously to all exposed parts of your body, and reapply regularly. Consider it your protective "clothing" against UV rays.

Stay Hydrated: Keep a water bottle handy (perhaps in that tool belt mentioned earlier). Staying hydrated is crucial, especially if you're gardening under the sun and sans clothes, as you might not notice just how much you're sweating.

Tool Maintenance: Keep your tools in good condition. Regularly clean them to prevent rust and deterioration, which can lead to unexpected breaks or malfunctions while in use. Well-maintained tools are safer tools.

Ergonomics: Pay attention to how you use your tools. Use proper form to avoid strains or injuries. Bend at the knees, keep your back straight, and avoid overreaching or twisting awkwardly, especially when handling heavy or unwieldy equipment.

Let me tell you, gardening in the nude is an absolute hoot, and before you think I've sprouted an extra flower stalk, hear me out. Imagine the sheer, unbridled joy of squishing cool mud between your toes, the sun warming your back, and a breeze that tickles just about everywhere. It's like being a part of your very own cheeky nature documentary—minus the camera crew and the awkward questions about bird mating dances.

Now, why is nude gardening so much fun? Well, for starters, there's something hilariously empowering about wielding a watering can with nothing on. It's like, "Look at me, hydrating hydrangeas and flaunting freedom, all at once!" And let's not forget the practical perks—no more grass stains or ruined clothes. Plus, laundry day becomes a breeze. Seriously, the clothes I wear to garden are none, so my washing machine is practically collecting cobwebs.

There's also a delightful element of surprise in nude gardening. Ever chased a runaway tomato rolling down the hill in the buff? It's an adrenaline rush that no clothed pursuit could ever match. And talk about getting in touch with your roots! There's no barrier between you and the earth. Every texture, temperature, and tremble of the earth feels magnified, like Mother Nature's giving you a high-five.

But perhaps the best part is the comedy of errors that inevitably unfolds. Ever misjudged the distance to a rose bush while in your birthday suit? Ouch, right? Or the first time you realize that sitting directly on the soil after a rain can be... quite the muddy surprise. It's these moments that add a layer of humor and humility to my gardening escapades.

Gardening nude isn't just about growing plants; it's about growing laughter and stories. Each gardening session is an episode in a sitcom where I'm both the star and the audience, laughing as I accidentally water my feet more than the ferns, or when I do a little dance to dodge a bee—because let's face it, some flowers aren't meant for buzzing visitors!

What If Your Neighbors See You?

There's this funny story that I have to share with you.

What if your neighbors see you? Ah, that's the perennial question for us nudist gardeners, isn't it? It's like playing a very risqué game of peek-a-boo—except you're not the one peeking, and you're definitely not hiding! Let me share a particularly memorable moment when my neighbor Joy got an unexpected eyeful.

It was a bright and sunny morning, perfect for some nude gardening. I was in the midst of liberating some carrots from the tyrannical grasp of weeds when I heard a gasp. Spinning around, a bit too quickly for comfort, I found myself face-to-face with Joy, my neighbor from two doors down. Her eyes were wide as saucers, and her mouth was forming words that seemed to have lost their way to her voice.

"Kristin!" she finally squeaked, her voice an octave higher than usual. "What on earth are you doing?"

I straightened up, hands on hips (carefully positioned to cover a bit of modesty), and gave her my most reassuring smile. "Morning, Joy! Just doing a bit of gardening."

"In the nude?!" Joy's voice could have startled the crows away for miles.

I chuckled, trying to ease the tension. "Yes, it's quite liberating! You feel every breeze, every bit of sunshine. It's all very natural and healthy!"

"But... but what if someone sees?" Joy looked around nervously, as though expecting a crowd to appear.

I shrugged, still smiling. "Well, it's just us and the carrots here, and they're not complaining. Besides, it's my little sanctuary here. I've got the fence and the hedge—pretty private, don't you think?"

Joy blinked, taking a moment to look around, her shock slowly subsiding as she noticed the high fences and thick greenery shielding my garden. "I... suppose so. But isn't it... awkward?"

"Only if you make it awkward, Joy. It's all about being comfortable in your own skin. Literally!" I laughed, hoping to break through her reservations.

She hesitated, then a small smile twitched at the corner of her mouth. "Well, I must admit, it does look rather... freeing. But it's not for me, dear. I'll stick to my gardening gloves and hat, thank you."

"We all have our styles, Joy. Mine just involves a bit less fabric!"

As she walked away, still shaking her head but chuckling now, I felt a swell of pride. Standing there, amidst my beloved plants, I wasn't just a naked gardener; I was a champion of freedom and fun in gardening.

A few days after the carrot-weeding incident, there was a knock at my door that sounded suspiciously like the opening beats of a courtroom drama. I opened the door to find Joy, flanked by her friends Michelle and Lea. Before I could even offer a cheery hello, the trio barged in, looking like they were ready to hold a town hall meeting in my living room.

"Kristin," Joy started, her voice firm, "we need to talk about this gardening... situation."

Michelle chimed in, arms crossed, "Yes, it's just not normal, Kristin. People are starting to talk."

Lea, who I knew only by the wave and a smile over the years, added, "And not just us. It's becoming a neighborhood issue."

I blinked, a bit taken aback by the sudden intervention but managed to keep my composure. "Well, come on in," I said, motioning to the sofa. "Let's talk about it. Can I get anyone some tea? Coffee?"

"No, thank you," they chorused, still standing.

Alright, straight to business then. I leaned against the counter, my expression open and friendly. "I understand it's unusual, but as I mentioned to Joy, my garden is quite private. I take measures to ensure I'm not visible to the public."

"But it's about decency, Kristin!" Michelle interjected. "What if kids see? Or what if someone takes a picture?"

I nodded, acknowledging their concerns. "I appreciate where you're coming from, really. But I've made sure that my garden is not visible from the street or any of the neighboring properties without, well, quite deliberate spying. As for kids, the fences are high, and there's dense foliage. Plus, this is my private property, and I'm within my legal rights to garden how I please."

Lea seemed a bit uncertain, her initial fervor cooling off. "I suppose we haven't actually seen anything from the street..."

Joy, still looking troubled, asked, "But why do you have to do it naked?"

I smiled, taking a moment to choose my words. "For me, it's more than just gardening. It's about being one with nature, feeling liberated, and frankly, enjoying the privacy of my own home. It's peaceful, it's therapeutic, and it harms no one."

Seeing them somewhat receptive, I offered a little more, "Why don't you come over for a BBQ this weekend? You can see the setup, and I promise, I'll be fully clothed. It'll be a chance to show you how secluded my garden really is."

"I don't think so!" Joy shouted back.

As they stood there, still a bit stern and skeptical, I decided to try one last time. "Why don't you come over for a BBQ this weekend? You can see the setup, and I promise, I'll be fully clothed. It'll be a chance to show you how secluded my garden really is."

Joy, however, dismissed the idea with a wave of her hand. "A BBQ? No, Kristin, that's not necessary. In fact, I have a better idea. Why don't you just strip naked right here, right now? Show Michelle and Lea exactly what you've been up to."

I laughed, thinking she must be joking. "Are you sure, Joy?"

Joy's expression didn't falter. "Yes, do it."

Well, if that's what it took to ease their minds, who was I to deny them? I grinned and began unbuttoning my shirt, feeling a mix of amusement and defiance. "Alright then," I said, slipping out of my clothes piece by piece until I stood completely naked in front of them.

I extended my arms, giving them the full view—boobs, butt, and everything in between. "Well, here I am! This is what your carrots and tomatoes see every morning."

Michelle's eyes widened, and Lea turned a shade of pink I'd only seen in blooming peonies. Joy, however, stayed focused, her stern look softening just a bit.

"So, what do you think?" I asked, doing a little twirl. "Is it really so scandalous?"

Lea finally broke the silence with a small, nervous laugh. "I have to admit, you look very... comfortable."

Michelle, still a bit shell-shocked, managed a nod. "And it does seem very... natural."

Joy sighed, her shoulders dropping a bit. "Alright, Kristin. You've made your point. We just wanted to understand. We don't need the whole neighborhood in a tizzy over something they don't even see."

I nodded, still standing there in my natural glory. "Exactly. It's all about personal comfort and freedom, without imposing on anyone else."

Joy finally cracked a smile. "You really are something, Kristin."

"And so are you, Joy. Now, about that BBQ? Fully clothed, of course."

The tension in the room dissolved into chuckles as I began to redress, feeling a sense of victory not just for my garden but for the understanding we'd cultivated that day.

The Basics of Gardening

Welcome to the heart and soul of our gardening adventure: the basics. Whether you're a seasoned horticulturist or a green-thumbed newbie, this chapter is your trusty trowel, ready to dig into the essentials of growing your own garden. And, of course, we'll be doing it all in our birthday suits because why not make the basics a bit more exhilarating?

Gardening, at its core, is about connecting with the earth. But when you're gardening naked, that connection becomes literal, immediate, and oh-so liberating. There's something profoundly satisfying about feeling the soil underfoot, the sun on your back, and the wind where the sun doesn't usually shine. Trust me, your plants will sense your freedom and grow all the better for it!

But before we start planting our naked dreams, we need to lay down some groundwork—pun intended. We'll cover everything from understanding your soil to picking the perfect plants for your garden. It's like dating, but with fewer awkward conversations and more dirt under your fingernails.

First, let's talk soil. It's the foundation of your garden, much like a good sense of humor is the foundation of our naked gardening escapades. We'll explore how to assess your soil type, improve its fertility, and create the perfect bed for your plants to thrive. And yes, we'll do it all while embracing the breeze.

Next, we'll dive into plant selection. Choosing the right plants is crucial; it's like choosing the right outfit for a night out, except here we're choosing nothing but the best for our garden. We'll look at climate-appropriate selections, easy-to-grow favorites, and some quirky options that will make your garden the talk of the nudist colony.

Of course, no garden is complete without proper planting techniques. We'll get down and dirty with seeds, seedlings, and transplants, ensuring you know exactly how to give your plants the best start in life. And since you're already naked, you might as well embrace the messiness—because gardening is never a clean affair, especially when you're doing it in the nude.

Soil 101

Alright, my fellow free spirits, let's get down to the nitty-gritty—literally. Soil is the foundation of any garden, and understanding it is the first step toward cultivating a lush, thriving paradise. Whether you're growing tomatoes or tulips, knowing your soil is like knowing your dance partner: it makes the whole experience smoother, more enjoyable, and much more productive. And yes, we'll be doing all of this while feeling the earth directly underfoot and elsewhere. Let's dive into Soil 101, shall we?

First things first, let's figure out what kind of soil you're working with. Soil comes in three basic types: sandy, clay, and loamy. Each has its own personality, much like your neighbors but with fewer opinions about your nudist lifestyle. To determine your soil type, grab a handful and give it a good squeeze. If it falls apart immediately, you've got sandy soil—great for drainage but can dry out faster than you can say "naked gardening." If it holds its shape but feels sticky, you've got clay soil, which retains water but can become compacted. If it forms a nice, crumbly ball, congratulations, you've got loamy soil, the goldilocks of gardening soils.

No matter what type of soil you have, there's always room for improvement. Think of it like giving your garden a facial—it's all about the quality of the dirt. For sandy soil, add organic matter like compost or well-rotted manure to help it retain moisture. Clay soil benefits from the same treatment, as organic matter helps break up the dense particles, improving drainage and aeration. If you're lucky enough to have loamy soil, keep adding compost to maintain its excellent structure and fertility. Just remember, naked or not, composting is your garden's best friend.

Next, we need to talk pH. Your soil's pH level affects nutrient availability for your plants. Most plants prefer a slightly acidic to neutral pH (around 6.0 to 7.0). You can test your soil's pH with a simple home test kit or send a sample to a local extension service. If your soil is too acidic (pH below 6.0), add lime to raise the pH. If it's too alkaline (pH above 7.0), add sulfur to lower it. Adjusting soil pH can take time, so be patient. Just like perfecting your tan, achieving the right pH balance is worth the wait.

Healthy soil is like a well-stocked pantry for your plants. Essential nutrients include nitrogen (for leafy growth), phosphorus (for roots and flowers), and potassium (for overall health). Adding compost or organic fertilizers can help replenish these nutrients. Cover crops, like clover or vetch, can also enrich your soil. Plant them in the off-season, and when they're tilled under, they add valuable organic matter and nutrients. Plus, they look charmingly rustic—just the vibe we're going for in our au naturel garden.

Maintaining your soil is an ongoing process. Regularly add organic matter to keep it fertile and well-structured. Mulch your garden beds to conserve moisture, suppress weeds, and slowly add nutrients as it decomposes. And don't forget to rotate your crops each season to prevent soil depletion and reduce pest issues. Remember, part of the joy of naked gardening is feeling the earth beneath your feet (and other parts). As you work the soil, embrace the sensation of the dirt on your skin. It's grounding, quite literally, and connects you to your garden in a uniquely intimate way.

Plant Selection

When it comes to naked gardening, plant selection is more than just picking pretty flowers and tasty veggies—it's about choosing flora that will thrive in your specific conditions while keeping your delicate, exposed skin in mind. After all, nobody wants to be running from a cactus or dealing with the sting of nettles while in the buff! So, let's dive into the fun and practical aspects of selecting the perfect plants for your nude garden.

First, consider your climate. Just like how some of us are more comfortable in tropical climates while others prefer a dry heat, plants have their own preferences too. Look for plants that are well-suited to your region's weather patterns, soil type, and sunlight levels. If you live in a hot, arid area, succulents, and drought-resistant plants will be your best friends. For cooler, wetter climates, think about hardy perennials and moisture-loving plants.

Next, think about the maintenance level you're comfortable with—both in terms of your gardening expertise and your tolerance for bending and reaching in all your naked glory. If you're new to gardening or just want to keep things simple, start with easy-to-grow plants like tomatoes, lettuce, and marigolds. These plants are forgiving, low-maintenance, and give you a satisfying yield with relatively little effort.

When choosing plants, also consider how they interact with your naked skin. Avoid plants with thorns, spines, or irritating oils. Roses may look beautiful, but they can be quite the prickly companion for a nude gardener. Opt for soft, lush plants that are a joy to brush against, like lavender, basil, and mint. These not only feel great but also smell divine, adding a sensory pleasure to your gardening experience.

Companion planting is another great strategy. By choosing plants that benefit each other when grown together, you can create a thriving ecosystem with minimal effort. For example, planting marigolds with tomatoes can help deter pests naturally, reducing the need for chemical interventions. Plus, it's a wonderful way to make your garden look vibrant and full of life, just like you!

Herbs are fantastic choices for a naked garden. They're generally easy to grow, require little space, and can be used in your cooking, adding a fresh, homegrown flavor to your meals. Imagine plucking a sprig of rosemary or a handful of basil straight from your garden while enjoying the sun on your skin. It's a simple pleasure that makes the whole naked gardening experience even more rewarding.

Edible plants, in general, are a win-win. They provide food for your table and a fulfilling gardening experience. Think about growing a mix of vegetables, fruits, and berries. Strawberries, cherry tomatoes, and snap peas are fun to grow and even more fun to snack on straight from the vine. Just be mindful of where you plant them—berries can stain if you accidentally sit on them, and nobody wants a blueberry tattoo on their behind!

Lastly, don't forget the aesthetics. A well-designed garden is a feast for the eyes and a source of immense pride. Mix different colors, textures, and heights to create a visually appealing space. Consider adding some ornamental grasses or flowering shrubs to give your garden structure and beauty throughout the year. And remember, a garden isn't just about the plants—it's about creating a space that makes you happy and reflects your personality.

In essence, plant selection for a nude garden is about finding the perfect balance between practicality and pleasure. Choose plants that thrive in your environment, are easy to care for, and bring you joy both visually and sensorially. With the right choices, your garden will be a paradise that's as enjoyable to tend as it is to relax in, all while embracing the freedom of gardening in the nude. So, strip down, get planting, and let your garden—and your spirit—bloom!

Planting Techniques

Alright, my fellow bare gardeners, it's time to get down and dirty—literally! Planting techniques are the backbone of a thriving garden, and doing it naked adds an extra layer of fun and connection with the earth. Let's dive into the essentials of planting, from seeds to seedlings, ensuring your garden flourishes while you enjoy the liberating experience of gardening in the buff.

First, let's talk seeds. There's something almost magical about planting seeds and watching them sprout into beautiful plants. To start, you'll need to prepare your soil. Remember our soil 101? Make sure it's well-aerated and enriched with compost. Use a garden fork or your hands (gloved or otherwise) to turn the soil and remove any debris. Feel free to revel in the sensation of the cool earth between your fingers and toes—it's one of the joys of naked gardening!

Once your soil is ready, it's time to sow the seeds. Follow the instructions on the seed packet regarding depth and spacing. Generally, you can plant seeds about twice as deep as their diameter. If you're not sure, a good rule of thumb is to plant them about a quarter to half an inch deep. For small seeds, you can simply sprinkle them on the surface and lightly cover them with soil. Gently press down to ensure good contact between the seed and soil.

Watering is crucial at this stage. Use a gentle spray to moisten the soil without washing the seeds away. Keep the soil consistently damp until the seeds germinate. This is the perfect time to soak up the sun and enjoy the warmth on your skin as you nurture your future plants. Just remember to apply sunscreen if you're spending a lot of time in direct sunlight—no one wants a sunburned nudist!

For those of you planting seedlings or transplants, the process is slightly different but just as enjoyable. Start by digging a hole twice as wide and just as deep as the root ball of your plant. Carefully remove the plant from its pot, being mindful not to damage the roots. Place it in the hole, ensuring it's at the same depth it was in the pot. Gently backfill the hole with soil, pressing lightly to eliminate air pockets.

After planting, give your new transplants a good drink of water. This helps settle the soil around the roots and gives the plant a strong start. As you water, take a moment to appreciate the sight and feel of the water soaking into the soil—there's something deeply satisfying about seeing your plants well-watered and happy.

Spacing is another important factor. Crowded plants compete for resources and are more susceptible to pests and diseases. Follow the spacing recommendations on seed packets or plant labels. If you're planting a row, use a string or a garden line to keep it straight. For a more natural look, plant in clusters or groups. This can make your garden look fuller and more aesthetically pleasing while still giving each plant enough room to thrive.

Mulching is your friend here. A layer of mulch helps retain moisture, suppress weeds, and improve soil fertility as it decomposes. Organic mulches like straw, grass clippings, or wood chips are great options. Spread a layer of mulch around your plants, being careful not to pile it against the stems, which can cause rot. Mulching while naked means you might get a bit of mulch in unexpected places, but that's part of the fun, right?

Now, let's talk about some advanced techniques. Companion planting is a fantastic way to maximize your garden's health and productivity. Pair plants that benefit each other, like tomatoes with basil or carrots with onions. This not only improves growth but can also deter pests and improve flavor. And when you're gardening naked, it's easy to move around and position yourself to plant just right without worrying about getting your clothes dirty.

Another technique to consider is succession planting. This involves planting crops in intervals to ensure a continuous harvest throughout the growing season. For example, after harvesting early crops like radishes or lettuce, you can replant the space with a later crop like beans or squash. This keeps your garden productive and provides a steady supply of fresh produce.

As you work, remember to enjoy the process. Gardening naked is about more than just growing plants—it's about connecting with nature in a primal, uninhibited way. Feel the sun on your back, the breeze on your skin, and the earth beneath your feet. Embrace the freedom and let it enhance your gardening experience.

Companion Planting

Just as you might appreciate a buddy to share sunscreen duties, your plants also benefit from friendly neighbors. Let's dive into the art and science of companion planting, making your garden not just a feast for the eyes, but a thriving, cooperative community.

Companion planting is all about pairing plants that enhance each other's growth and health. Some plants provide natural pest control, others improve soil fertility, and some simply make their neighbors grow better. It's like matchmaking for plants, and when done right, it can transform your garden into a paradise of productivity and beauty.

Let's start with the classic trio: corn, beans, and squash, often referred to as the "Three Sisters." This ancient planting method was used by Native Americans and showcases the magic of companion planting. Corn provides a natural trellis for the beans to climb, beans fix nitrogen in the soil, enriching it for the corn and squash, and the sprawling squash leaves act as a living mulch, suppressing weeds and conserving moisture. It's a win-win-win situation that makes you wonder why anyone would plant them separately!

Next up, let's talk about basil and tomatoes—a match made in heaven. Basil not only enhances the flavor of tomatoes but also repels pests like aphids, whiteflies, and tomato hornworms. Plus, having fresh basil and tomatoes growing together means caprese salad is always just a few steps away. Imagine harvesting these fragrant, delicious plants while enjoying the sun on your bare skin—pure bliss!

Marigolds are another superstar in the companion planting world. Their bright, cheerful flowers not only add a pop of color to your garden but also deter a wide range of pests, including nematodes and aphids. Plant marigolds around your vegetable beds or interspersed with crops like lettuce, beans, and tomatoes. Their pest-repelling properties will keep your garden healthy, and their beauty will keep your spirits high.

Speaking of lettuce, let's pair it with radishes and carrots. Radishes grow quickly and help break up the soil, making it easier for carrots to grow. Lettuce provides a natural ground cover, helping to retain soil moisture and suppress weeds. Plus, the different growth rates mean you'll have a continuous harvest—radishes ready in a few weeks, lettuce in a couple of months, and carrots taking their time to become sweet and crunchy.

Onions and garlic are fantastic companions for many plants, particularly strawberries and carrots. Their strong smell deters pests, including aphids and carrot flies. Planting onions or garlic around the edges of your garden beds can create a natural pest barrier, protecting your more delicate plants from harm. And think of the delicious culinary combinations you can create with fresh garden produce!

Beans, whether bush or pole, are excellent companions for a variety of crops, particularly heavy feeders like corn, broccoli, and cabbage. Beans fix nitrogen in the soil, providing essential nutrients for their companions. Plus, their climbing nature means they can share space with taller plants, maximizing your garden's productivity.

Of course, there are some pairings to avoid, much like how you wouldn't mix white wine with red meat. For example, keep fennel away from most plants as it tends to inhibit their growth. Similarly, avoid planting onions near beans and peas, as they can stunt each other's development.

As you plan your garden, think about the relationships between your plants. Companion planting is about creating a balanced ecosystem where each plant contributes to the overall health of the garden. It's like a nudist potluck where everyone brings their best dish—each contribution makes the whole experience better.

In your naked gardening endeavors, companion planting offers the added benefit of reducing the need for chemical pesticides and fertilizers. By letting nature take its course, you can enjoy a healthier, more organic garden. Plus, the closer connection with your plants—literally and figuratively—enhances the overall joy of gardening in the nude.

Another Hilarious Story

Let me tell you about a day in the garden that Landon and I will never forget. It was one of those absolutely perfect days—clear skies, warm sun, and the perfect temperature to enjoy the liberating feeling of gardening in the nude. Landon, with his chiseled physique, looked like a Greek statue come to life as he tended to our tomatoes. I couldn't help but admire him, feeling a blend of love and pride for my handsome boyfriend.

We were deep into our work, enjoying the tactile pleasure of the soil and the breeze on our bare skin, when suddenly, from the corner of my eye, I noticed a flash of movement. I turned just in time to see Joy, our ever-curious neighbor, peering over the fence with her phone in hand, snapping a photo.

"Aha!" Joy exclaimed triumphantly, capturing our attention and freezing us in our tracks.

Before we could react, Joy had already sent the photo.

A few hours later, Landon and I were chilling in the living room of the home nude, and there was a knock on our door. Not just any knock, but the kind that suggested a blend of urgency and excitement. I sighed, knowing exactly what was coming.

Opening the door, I found Joy, Michelle, and Lea standing there, clearly having seen the photo.

"Kristin!" Joy began, her tone a mix of indignation and amusement. "We saw the photo and just had to come over."

Still in my gardening apron, I couldn't help but laugh. "Joy, Michelle, Lea, what a surprise. Come on in."

They didn't need a second invitation. The three women barged in, eyes wide with curiosity and a touch of admiration.

Michelle, unable to contain herself, said, "I have to say, Kristin, Landon certainly is... well-built."

Lea nodded enthusiastically, "Yes, quite the form indeed."

We were back inside the house after Joy's impromptu photo session when Joy, Michelle, and Lea decided they wanted a closer look. Joy, always the bold one, pointed directly at Landon.

"Landon, take off that apron. We need to see the full picture."

Landon looked at me, and I shrugged with a mischievous smile. "Go on, Landon. They've come all this way."

With a deep breath and a playful grin, Landon untied the apron and let it fall to the floor, standing confidently in his natural state. The women gasped, not out of shock, but out of sheer appreciation.

"Wow," Michelle said, eyes wide. "You really do have quite the garden... and gardener."

Lea giggled, "I think we need to start calling this place Eden."

Then, in a surprising turn of events, they decided to inspect Landon more closely. Joy, ever the ringleader, gave his penis a thorough look and announced, "I give it an A."

Lea, slightly more reserved but clearly impressed, said, "A- for me. Almost perfect."

Michelle, always the more critical eye, nodded thoughtfully, "Solid B. Very respectable."

I stood there, beaming with pride. Landon took their appraisals with good humor, standing tall and unashamed. It was an odd, yet oddly liberating moment for all of us.

As we started to settle back into normal conversation, Michelle suddenly announced, "Well, Kristin, we've decided we're staying over. We need to see more of this lifestyle, and frankly, I don't care if it's your house."

I blinked, caught off guard but amused by her boldness. "Alright then, ladies. Make yourselves at home. Just remember, here in our little paradise, clothes are entirely optional."

As the initial shock and amusement began to settle, the three girls made themselves comfortable in our living room. I decided to brew some tea, thinking it might help ease the transition into this unexpected nudist gathering. With mugs of steaming tea in hand, Joy, Michelle, and Lea settled onto the sofa, still chuckling about the afternoon's events.

Landon and I, feeling the playful energy in the air, exchanged a glance. I don't remember who started it, but before long, we were both humming a silly tune about gardening. One thing led to another, and soon we were dancing around the living room, completely nude, and singing about our love for gardening. It was like an impromptu musical number that we didn't even know we had inside us.

"Dancing through the daisies, feeling oh-so free,
Naked in the garden, just you and me!"

Landon twirled me around, and we both laughed as we made up verses on the spot.

"Planting in the sunshine, bare feet on the ground,
In our little Eden, joy is all around!"

The girls watched us, eyes wide and laughter bubbling up as they sipped their tea. Joy, ever the critic, clapped her hands in delight.

"Bravo! This is better than any TV show!"

Lea nodded, wiping tears of laughter from her eyes. "You two are something else!"

Michelle, usually the most reserved, was laughing so hard she could barely keep her tea in her cup. "I never thought I'd see this today. You guys are amazing!"

We danced and sang, twirling and dipping, turning our living room into a stage for our garden-themed performance. It was silly, spontaneous, and absolutely wonderful. There was something so freeing about sharing this unfiltered joy with our neighbors, showing them just how fun and liberating our nudist lifestyle could be.

As the song wound down, we took a final bow, breathless and beaming. The girls applauded, their laughter filling the room. It was a moment of pure, unadulterated joy—one that none of us would soon forget.

Joy, always the spokesperson, raised her teacup in a toast. "To Kristin and Landon, the most delightful gardeners and entertainers we've ever met!"

We all clinked our cups together, basking in the camaraderie and the shared laughter. It was a perfect end to a day that had started with a simple gardening session and turned into an unforgettable celebration of freedom and friendship.

And as we settled into the evening, we knew this was just the beginning of many more adventures together, both in the garden and beyond.

Seasonal Naked Gardening

Gardening in the buff offers a unique way to experience the rhythms of nature throughout the year. Each season brings its own set of joys and challenges, transforming your garden and your gardening habits in delightful and unexpected ways.

Imagine feeling the first warmth of spring sunshine on your bare skin after a long, cold winter. There's nothing quite like it. Spring is a time of renewal and rebirth, and as you shed your winter layers, you can't help but feel a sense of connection to the new growth sprouting all around you. We'll explore the best ways to prepare your garden—and yourself—for the busy planting season ahead.

Summer takes the naked gardening experience to its peak. The long, hot days are perfect for soaking up the sun while tending to your flourishing plants. It's a season of abundance and vitality, where your hard work starts to pay off with bountiful harvests. However, summer also requires extra precautions to protect your skin from the intense sun. We'll cover everything from strategic sunbathing to hydration tips that ensure you and your garden thrive.

Autumn is a time of transition, where the garden slows down and prepares for the rest period of winter. The cooler temperatures make working outside in the nude incredibly refreshing. There's a sense of satisfaction in harvesting the last of your crops and putting the garden to bed. We'll guide you through the best practices for fall gardening, including composting and preparing your soil for next year's growth.

Winter, for most, might seem like the end of naked gardening. But fear not! Even in the colder months, there are ways to stay connected to your garden. Whether it's planning next year's layout, starting seeds indoors, or braving a brisk day to check on winter crops, we'll help you find joy and purpose in your garden year-round.

Winter

Winter might seem like the end of the naked gardening season, but don't hang up your trowel just yet! While it's true that the cold can put a damper on extended outdoor activities, there are still plenty of ways to stay connected to your garden—and yes, even enjoy a bit of naked time if you're brave and properly prepared. Winter is a time for planning, preparation, and a few chilly but invigorating garden tasks.

First, let's talk about planning. Winter is the perfect time to dream big for the coming year. Cozy up inside with a warm drink and sketch out your garden plans. Research new plants you want to try, map out your crop rotations, and decide on any structural changes you'd like to make to your garden. This is the season to let your imagination run wild while staying snug and warm.

But what about those days when you crave a bit of outdoor time, even if it's brisk? There are still a few tasks you can tackle in your garden, provided you bundle up—though maybe not in your usual garden attire. Think layers of cozy sweaters and a good pair of gloves. For the truly adventurous, a quick, invigorating check on your winter crops can be an exhilarating experience. Just be sure to limit your exposure and head back inside before you turn into a human popsicle.

Winter crops like kale, Brussels sprouts, and certain types of cabbage can withstand colder temperatures and often taste sweeter after a frost. Harvesting these hardy vegetables can give you a reason to venture out, even on the chilliest days. There's a special kind of satisfaction that comes from picking fresh produce in the depths of winter, knowing that your garden is still providing for you.

Indoor gardening is another fantastic way to keep your green thumb active during the winter months. Setting up a small indoor herb garden on a sunny windowsill can bring a touch of summer into your home. Basil, mint, and parsley are all excellent choices for indoor growing. Plus, they add fresh flavors to your winter meals and a bit of greenery to your indoor space.

Winter is also the time to focus on maintaining and preparing your tools for the next growing season. Clean, sharpen, and oil your garden tools so they're ready to go when the ground thaws. It's a task that doesn't require much time outdoors and can be done in a shed or garage, where you can work comfortably bundled up.

Composting is another activity that doesn't stop just because it's cold. Keep adding kitchen scraps to your compost pile or bin, and give it a turn whenever you can. Decomposition slows down in the winter, but it doesn't stop entirely. Come spring, you'll have rich compost ready to nourish your garden beds.

For those days when the call of the garden is just too strong, consider a greenhouse or cold frame. These structures can extend your growing season and provide a warm, sheltered space where you can enjoy some naked gardening even in winter. Imagine the delight of tending to plants in a cozy greenhouse while snow falls gently outside.

Spring

Ah, spring—the season of renewal, rebirth, and the delightful return to naked gardening. After the cold months of winter, there's nothing quite like shedding those extra layers and feeling the warm sun on your bare skin. Spring is when everything in the garden comes alive, and you, my fellow nudist gardener, get to be right there in the midst of it, basking in the glory of nature's awakening.

The first warm days of spring are magical. The sun feels warmer, the birds sing louder, and the air is filled with the sweet scent of blooming flowers and fresh earth. This is the time to prepare your garden beds, plant new seeds, and welcome the growing season with open arms—and no clothes. Trust me, there's no better way to celebrate the end of winter than by getting down and dirty in your garden.

Start by giving your garden a thorough spring cleaning. Remove any debris that accumulated over the winter—dead leaves, fallen branches, and any weeds that dared to survive the cold. This is also a great time to turn your compost pile, incorporating the decomposed material into your garden beds to enrich the soil. There's something deeply satisfying about feeling the cool, rich soil between your fingers (and toes) as you prepare it for new plantings.

Next, focus on soil preparation. After a long winter, your soil will benefit from a good refresh. Add compost or well-rotted manure to boost fertility and improve soil structure. Use a garden fork or tiller to mix the organic matter into the soil, creating a nutrient-rich environment for your plants.

As you work, take a moment to enjoy the sensation of the earth beneath your bare feet—it's a grounding experience that connects you directly to the land.

Spring is the perfect time to start planting cool-season crops like lettuce, spinach, radishes, and peas. These hardy vegetables thrive in the mild temperatures of early spring and can often be harvested before the heat of summer sets in. Sow seeds directly into the prepared soil, following the instructions on the seed packets for depth and spacing. Water them gently, and watch as the first green shoots begin to appear.

Don't forget about flowers! Spring bulbs like tulips, daffodils, and crocuses add vibrant splashes of color to your garden and herald the arrival of warmer weather. If you planted bulbs in the fall, they should be popping up now, ready to brighten your garden. If not, consider adding some spring-blooming perennials to create a colorful, dynamic landscape that will come back year after year.

One of the joys of spring gardening is watching the wildlife return to your garden. Birds, bees, butterflies, and other pollinators begin to reappear, bringing life and movement to your outdoor space. Planting a variety of flowers and shrubs that attract these beneficial creatures will help ensure a healthy, thriving garden. Plus, it's a delight to watch them flit and buzz around you as you garden.

Spring is also the time to start thinking about your summer garden. Plan out your beds, deciding where to plant warm-season crops like tomatoes, peppers, and cucumbers once the danger of frost has passed. Starting seeds indoors can give you a head start on the growing season. Set up a seedling station with trays, grow lights, and a bit of indoor nudist gardening fun. There's nothing like watching your seedlings sprout and grow, knowing they'll soon be transplanted into your outdoor garden.

As the days grow longer and warmer, take advantage of the beautiful spring weather to enjoy your garden in all its glory. Spend time weeding, watering, and tending to your plants, reveling in the freedom of naked gardening. The cool morning air, the warmth of the midday sun, and the gentle breeze on your skin create a sensory experience that's both invigorating and peaceful.

Summer

Summer in the garden is a time of abundance, vibrancy, and the peak of the naked gardening experience. The days are long and warm, the plants are thriving, and there's a palpable sense of energy and life in the air. For a nudist gardener, summer offers the perfect conditions to enjoy the freedom of gardening in the buff, feeling the sun on your skin and the earth beneath your feet.

The first thing to remember about summer gardening is that hydration is key—both for you and your plants. The intense summer sun can quickly dry out soil, so regular watering is essential. Early morning or late evening is the best time to water your garden, as it reduces evaporation and gives your plants a chance to absorb moisture before the heat of the day. Plus, these cooler parts of the day are also the most comfortable times to be out in the garden naked, avoiding the risk of sunburn or overheating.

Speaking of sunburn, sunscreen becomes your best friend in the summer. Apply a broad-spectrum sunscreen generously to all exposed skin, and reapply regularly, especially if you're sweating or spending extended periods outside. A wide-brimmed hat and sunglasses can also help protect your face and eyes while adding a touch of style to your nude gardening ensemble.

As you water your plants, take the time to enjoy the sensory experience of gardening nude. The cool splash of water on your skin, the warmth of the sun, and the gentle breeze all combine to create a uniquely refreshing feeling. It's a wonderful way to stay connected with nature and truly feel a part of your garden.

Summer is the season of growth, and your garden should be bursting with life. Tomatoes, peppers, cucumbers, and other warm-season crops will be reaching their peak. Regularly check your plants for signs of pests or diseases, and address any issues promptly to keep your garden healthy. Companion planting, like basil with tomatoes or marigolds with just about anything, can help deter pests naturally, making your gardening experience more enjoyable and less labor-intensive.

Weeding is another important task during the summer months. Weeds compete with your plants for water and nutrients, so keeping them under control is crucial. Hand-weeding can be a meditative activity, especially when done in the nude. Feel the texture of the soil and the plants as you work, and enjoy the satisfaction of a tidy, well-maintained garden.

Mulching is a great way to conserve moisture, suppress weeds, and regulate soil temperature. Organic mulches like straw, wood chips, or grass clippings can be spread around your plants to create a protective barrier. Not only does this help your garden thrive, but it also feels wonderful to walk on a mulched path with bare feet.

Harvesting your summer crops is one of the most rewarding aspects of gardening. There's nothing quite like picking a ripe tomato or a crisp cucumber straight from the vine and enjoying it right there in the garden. The flavors are more intense, and the experience of eating food you've grown yourself, while basking in the sun, is incredibly fulfilling. Just be sure to wash your produce before eating to remove any dirt or bugs that might have hitched a ride.

Summer also brings opportunities for preserving the bounty of your garden. Canning, drying, and freezing are excellent ways to extend the life of your harvest and enjoy the taste of summer long after the season has passed. Setting up a little outdoor processing station can be a fun way to keep the mess out of the kitchen and enjoy the warm weather.

Remember to take breaks and stay cool. A small kiddie pool or a garden hose can provide a refreshing way to cool down on hot days. Splashing around in the water, feeling the sun and breeze on your skin, is pure summer bliss. It's also a great way to rinse off any dirt and grime from your gardening adventures.

Autumn

Autumn is a magical time in the garden, a season of transition where the vibrant energy of summer gives way to the cooler, more reflective days of fall. For the naked gardener, it's a time to enjoy the refreshing crispness in the air while preparing the garden for winter. There's a special kind of beauty in autumn gardening, where the golden light and changing leaves create a stunning backdrop for your nude gardening adventures.

The first task in autumn is to harvest the last of your summer crops. Tomatoes, peppers, and other warm-season vegetables will be coming to the end of their production, and now is the time to gather the final fruits of your labor. There's a deep sense of satisfaction in this, knowing that your garden has provided so abundantly throughout the summer. As you pick the last ripe tomatoes and peppers, feel the cool autumn air on your skin and savor the moment.

After harvesting, it's time to clean up the garden. Remove spent plants, dead leaves, and any other debris that could harbor pests or diseases over the winter. Compost healthy plant material, but discard any that show signs of disease to prevent it from spreading. This cleanup process can be quite enjoyable when done in the nude, as the cool air invigorates you and the autumn sun warms your back.

Next, consider planting cover crops or green manures. These plants, like clover, rye, or vetch, help protect and enrich your soil over the winter. They prevent erosion, add organic matter, and can fix nitrogen in the soil. Sowing cover crops in the fall ensures that your garden beds are ready for a strong start in the spring. Plus, the sight of green seedlings sprouting in the crisp autumn air is a delightful reminder that life continues even as the seasons change.

Autumn is also an excellent time for planting bulbs and perennials. Spring-flowering bulbs like tulips, daffodils, and crocuses need to be planted now so they can establish roots before the ground freezes. Digging into the cool, moist soil while naked connects you deeply to the earth, and planting bulbs is a promise to yourself of the beauty to come. The simple act of placing each bulb into the ground, envisioning the colorful blooms of spring, is both grounding and uplifting.

Don't forget to mulch your garden beds. A layer of mulch helps regulate soil temperature, retain moisture, and protect plant roots from the cold. Organic mulches like straw, leaves, or wood chips are ideal. As you spread mulch around your plants, enjoy the sensory experience of handling natural materials and the satisfaction of tucking your garden in for the winter.

Autumn is also the time to prune back perennials and shrubs. Trim away dead or diseased branches and shape your plants to encourage healthy growth next season. Pruning can be a meditative activity, allowing you to reflect on the past growing season and plan for the future. The cool autumn air and the earthy scent of freshly cut branches enhance the experience, making it a peaceful and contemplative task.

As the days grow shorter and the nights cooler, take some time to enjoy your garden in its autumn glory. The golden light of late afternoon, the rustling of leaves, and the rich colors of fall create a serene and beautiful environment. Whether you're raking leaves, planting bulbs, or simply sitting quietly and enjoying the view, let yourself fully immerse in the sensory pleasures of the season.

One of the joys of autumn is the harvest of cool-season crops. Vegetables like kale, Brussels sprouts, and carrots often taste sweeter after a frost. Harvest these hardy crops and savor their fresh, crisp flavors. There's nothing like pulling a carrot from the cool soil or picking kale leaves on a brisk autumn morning, feeling the earth's energy in your hands and the cool air on your skin.

As you prepare your garden for the coming winter, take a moment to reflect on the past growing season. Celebrate your successes, learn from your challenges, and look forward to the next cycle of growth. Autumn is a time of closure and preparation, a season that invites you to connect deeply with the rhythms of nature.

Maintaining Your Garden...But Not Your Modesty

There's nothing quite like the blend of dirt, sun, and a breeze where the sun doesn't usually shine to keep you feeling alive and connected to nature. Now, let's get down to the nitty-gritty of keeping your garden in tip-top shape while you remain blissfully bare.

First off, let's talk about weeding. Weeds are the uninvited guests at your garden party, and they love to crash the scene. There's something wonderfully primal about pulling weeds while naked. You can feel every tug, every root snap, and when you toss those pesky invaders aside, it's like asserting your dominance over nature itself. Just watch out for the ones with thorns—learned that the hard way!

Watering is another essential task, and doing it in the nude adds a whole new dimension of fun. Early morning or late evening are the best times to water, not just for your plants but also to avoid sunburn on your more delicate parts. Plus, there's something quite liberating about holding a hose with nothing but a grin. Just try not to get too carried away with the water fights; neighbors have a way of appearing at the most inopportune moments.

Speaking of sunburn, sunscreen is your best friend. Apply it liberally and everywhere. Trust me, there's nothing funny about a sunburned butt. I once forgot to reapply after a long afternoon of planting, and let's just say, sitting was not pleasant for a few days. Now, I have a strict regimen: sunscreen, hat, sunglasses, and if it's really sunny, maybe a strategically placed garden gnome for extra shade.

Mulching is another task that's surprisingly satisfying when done nude. Spreading mulch around your plants helps retain moisture, suppress weeds, and gives your garden a tidy, well-cared-for look. Plus, it feels amazing to walk barefoot on a freshly mulched path. Just be careful with the wood chips—those splinters can find their way into places you definitely don't want them.

Pruning can be quite the art form. It's like giving your plants a haircut, and when you're doing it naked, you might feel like a sculptor in their studio, every snip bringing your garden closer to perfection. Just be mindful of where the clippings fall—stepping on a thorny branch with bare feet is not my idea of fun.

Fertilizing, whether with compost or store-bought products, is essential for a healthy garden. Turning compost in the nude is a full sensory experience. The smell of rich, decomposed organic matter, the warmth of the compost pile, and the feel of the earth beneath your feet—it's practically therapeutic. Just remember to wash thoroughly afterward. Compost is great for plants, not so much for humans.

One of my favorite maintenance tasks is deadheading flowers. It's a simple job: just snip off the spent blooms to encourage new growth. It's meditative, and wandering through the garden with scissors in hand, nude as the day I was born, makes me feel like an eccentric artist, bringing beauty and order to my botanical masterpiece.

Pest control is where things can get a bit tricky. If you're dealing with a bug infestation, you might need to don some gloves, and maybe a bit more, depending on how aggressive the pests are. I once tackled an aphid problem on my roses with nothing but my birthday suit and a spray bottle of soapy water. The neighbors got quite the show, but hey, those roses were worth it!

Lastly, take time to simply enjoy your garden. Maintenance isn't all work and no play. Sit down, relax, and bask in the beauty of what you've created. Feel the sun on your skin, listen to the rustle of leaves, and breathe in the fresh air. Naked gardening isn't just about growing plants; it's about nurturing your own connection to the earth and reveling in the joy of being truly yourself.

Maintaining your garden without maintaining your modesty adds an extra layer of fun and freedom to your gardening routine. It's about feeling every part of the process, literally, and enjoying the cheeky delight of being one with nature. So, grab your tools (and maybe some sunscreen), and dive into the hilariously rewarding world of naked garden maintenance. Your plants will thank you, and you'll have a blast doing it!

How Landon and I Broke Up

Breaking up with Landon was one of those days you never quite forget, no matter how much you might want to. It started out as a normal day in our little slice of naked paradise. We were in the garden, of course, enjoying the freedom and the sun, when Landon turned to me with a serious look on his face.

"Kristin," he said, "we need to talk."

Now, "we need to talk" is never a good opener. I knew something was up, but I wasn't prepared for what came next.

"Last week, with Joy, Michelle, and Lea," he began, hesitating a bit, "it was fun, but I think it went too far. I mean, dancing naked and all... in front of them... it was a bit much."

I felt a pang in my chest. "What do you mean? We were having fun, they were laughing, and everyone seemed to be enjoying themselves. What's wrong with that?"

Landon sighed. "Kristin, I've been thinking about this for a while. It's not just that day. It's everything. The constant nudity, the lack of boundaries. I think you're too obsessed with being naked all the time."

His words stung. "Obsessed? I wouldn't call it that. I just enjoy the freedom. It's not about being naked for the sake of it; it's about feeling connected to nature, to myself. You used to enjoy it too."

"I do, but there's a limit," he replied, frustration creeping into his voice. "There's a time and place for everything. I can't shake the feeling that you're pushing this lifestyle onto everyone around you, and it's becoming too much."

We stood there, the garden suddenly feeling much smaller. "Landon, it's about more than just being naked. It's about being comfortable in your own skin, literally and figuratively. It's about not being confined by society's expectations. Don't you see that?"

He shook his head. "I get it, Kristin, I do. But there has to be a balance. I can't live every moment without clothes, worrying about who might see, or what they might think. It's exhausting. I want to enjoy life without feeling like I'm on display all the time."

His words hit hard. "So, what are you saying? That I should just cover up and conform?"

"I'm saying there needs to be a middle ground," he said softly. "But I don't think you're willing to find it. And I can't keep pretending that I'm okay with this when I'm not."

The silence that followed was heavy. I wanted to argue, to convince him that what we were doing was beautiful and freeing. But deep down, I knew this was about more than just nudity. It was about our different values, our different ways of living.

"Maybe you're right," I finally said, my voice shaking. "Maybe we are too different."

Landon nodded, looking both relieved and heartbroken. "I think so, Kristin. It doesn't mean I don't care about you. I just can't live this way anymore."

We stood there for what felt like an eternity, the garden that had once been our sanctuary now a place of painful realization. Eventually, he turned and walked away, leaving me standing there, bare and alone.

In the days that followed, I found myself questioning everything. Was I too obsessed? Had I pushed him too far? But as the initial hurt began to fade, I realized that I couldn't change who I was or what I believed in. Being naked was part of me, part of my identity and my joy.

Losing Landon was painful, but it also reaffirmed my commitment to living authentically. I still believe in the virtues of nudity, in the freedom and connection it brings. It's not for everyone, and that's okay. But for me, it's a way of life that I wouldn't trade for anything.

And so, the garden remains my sanctuary, a place where I can be truly myself, whether alone or with those who share my love for the naked truth.

The Body and Soul Benefits of Naked Gardening

Naked gardening allows your skin to breathe and soak up the natural elements in a way that clothing simply doesn't permit. The most obvious benefit here is the increased exposure to sunlight, which boosts your vitamin D levels. This essential vitamin is crucial for bone health, immune function, and overall mood. Just remember to apply sunscreen to avoid the infamous "gardener's burn" on parts of your body that aren't used to seeing the sun!

There's also the benefit of tactile sensation. Feeling the soil between your toes, the breeze on your skin, and the coolness of the water as you hose down your plants provides a full-body sensory experience that's both grounding and invigorating. This direct contact with the elements can improve circulation, enhance sensory awareness, and even stimulate the release of endorphins, those delightful hormones that make you feel happy and relaxed.

Naked gardening is a fantastic form of exercise, too. Bending, stretching, squatting, and lifting are all integral parts of tending to your garden, and doing it without clothes allows for a greater range of motion. You're more aware of your body's movements and posture, which can lead to better physical alignment and less strain on your joints and muscles. Plus, without the restriction of clothing, you might find yourself naturally moving more and stretching further, which is great for flexibility and strength.

Now, let's get to the heart of the matter: the soulful benefits of gardening in the nude. There's an undeniable sense of freedom and authenticity that comes with being naked in nature. It's a return to your natural state, free from societal expectations and the constraints of modern life. This sense of liberation fosters a deep connection to the earth and to yourself, encouraging mindfulness and a profound appreciation for the simple pleasures of life.

Naked gardening also promotes body positivity and self-acceptance. When you're out there, bare and unashamed, you're embracing your body as it is, in all its natural glory. This can be incredibly empowering, helping you to shed insecurities and develop a healthier relationship with your body. It's a practice in vulnerability and confidence, allowing you to appreciate the strength and beauty of your physical form while focusing on the nurturing act of gardening.

The meditative aspect of naked gardening cannot be overstated. The rhythmic tasks of planting, weeding, and harvesting become a form of moving meditation, allowing you to be fully present in the moment. The sensory engagement, combined with the peaceful environment of the garden, creates a perfect setting for mindfulness. As you connect with the earth, you're also connecting with your inner self, finding peace and clarity amidst the greenery.

There's also a wonderful sense of community that can come from naked gardening, especially if you're part of a group or club. Sharing this unique experience with others fosters a sense of camaraderie and mutual respect. You're all there, vulnerable and free, united by a common love for nature and the joy of being unencumbered. It's a beautiful reminder of our shared humanity and the simple pleasures that bring us together.

Lastly, let's not forget the joy and laughter that often accompanies naked gardening. There's a playful, childlike delight in being naked outdoors, and this sense of fun can lighten your mood and reduce stress. Whether it's the humor of a runaway tomato rolling down the hill or the spontaneous dance in the rain, these moments of joy are good for the soul, reminding you to take life a little less seriously and enjoy the present.

My Battle with Joy

The breakup with Landon was still fresh, and I couldn't shake the feeling that Joy had played a part in it. The incident with the photo and the ensuing nudist show for her, Michelle, and Lea kept replaying in my mind. I decided it was time to confront her, to get some answers and maybe, just maybe, some closure.

I walked over to Joy's house, my heart pounding. She answered the door with a cheerful smile that quickly faded when she saw the look on my face.

"Kristin, what's wrong?" she asked, concern etching her features.

"Can we talk?" I said, trying to keep my voice steady. She nodded and led me to her living room. I took a deep breath and dove right in. "Joy, I need to know—did you have anything to do with Landon breaking up with me?"

Joy looked taken aback. "What? Kristin, no! Why would you think that?"

"Because ever since that day in the garden, things have been different. Landon said I took things too far, that I'm too obsessed with nudity. He said he felt pushed into something he wasn't comfortable with, and I can't help but think that your reaction played a part in that."

Joy sighed and shook her head. "Kristin, I didn't mean to cause any trouble. Yes, we took that photo and had some fun, but it was all in good spirits. I never thought it would lead to this."

"Good spirits?" I retorted, feeling the frustration bubble up. "You and your friends barged in, demanded Landon strip in front of you, and then graded him like he was some sort of display. How did you think that would make him feel? How did you think it would make me feel?"

Joy's face hardened. "Kristin, you invited us in. You and Landon were the ones dancing naked and putting on a show. We didn't force you to do anything. If Landon felt uncomfortable, that's on him. And if you're so obsessed with being naked that you can't see how it affects others, maybe you need to look at yourself."

I could feel my anger rising, but I tried to keep it in check. "I enjoy being naked because it makes me feel free and connected to nature. I thought Landon understood that. But your actions, your judgments, they made him feel exposed in a way that wasn't freeing. It made him question everything."

Joy crossed her arms, her eyes narrowing. "Kristin, maybe Landon breaking up with you wasn't just about me or that one incident. Maybe he couldn't handle the lifestyle you want to live. And maybe, just maybe, you're blaming me because you don't want to face that truth."

Her words stung because deep down, I knew there was some truth to them. But I wasn't ready to admit it. "You still had no right to make him feel that way, Joy. You crossed a line, and it cost me someone I loved."

Joy's expression softened slightly. "I'm sorry, Kristin. I never intended for any of this to happen. But you need to understand that not everyone sees the world the way you do. Landon didn't leave because of me. He left because he couldn't reconcile your lifestyle with his own comfort levels."

We stood there in silence for a moment, the weight of her words sinking in. I realized that I had been looking for someone to blame because it was easier than accepting that Landon and I just weren't right for each other.

"Maybe you're right," I said quietly, feeling the fight drain out of me. "But it still hurts."

Joy reached out and squeezed my hand. "I know it does. And I'm truly sorry for any part I played in that hurt. I just hope you can find a way to move forward and keep being true to yourself."

I nodded, appreciating her words even though the pain was still fresh. "Thanks, Joy. I just needed to hear it from you."

We stood there for a few more moments, not as adversaries, but as neighbors trying to understand each other. It wasn't the closure I had hoped for, but it was a step towards healing. And maybe, in time, I'd find the balance between my love for nudity and the relationships that mattered most.

* * *

A few days after my confrontation with Joy, I found myself stewing over our conversation. The more I thought about it, the more I felt that I hadn't fully expressed how deeply her actions had impacted me. So, I decided to go back and confront her again. This time, I was determined to make my point crystal clear.

I marched over to Joy's house, my heart pounding with a mix of determination and apprehension. When I rang the doorbell, it was Michelle who answered, with Lea standing just behind her.

"Oh, Kristin," Michelle said with a raised eyebrow, "what brings you here?"

"I need to talk to Joy," I said firmly, trying to keep my voice steady.

Lea stepped forward, blocking the entrance. "What's this about, Kristin? Didn't you two already have a conversation?"

"It's not finished," I replied, my frustration bubbling up again. "I need to speak to her."

They exchanged a look, and then Michelle said, "Alright, but first, you need to do something for us."

I narrowed my eyes. "And what's that?"

Lea smirked. "Strip naked. Right here, right now."

I felt a flash of anger but also a strange sense of defiance. If they thought they could shame me or get the better of me by forcing me to strip, they were sorely mistaken. I straightened up and began to unbutton my shirt.

"You think you got the better of me, but I enjoy this!" I said, my voice ringing with conviction. "You can't shame me with something I love."

As I stripped off my clothes, piece by piece, I could see the surprise in their eyes. I stood there, completely bare, facing them down. "Now, where's Joy?" I demanded.

Michelle and Lea stepped aside, somewhat taken aback by my confidence. Joy appeared at the doorway, her expression a mix of surprise and curiosity.

"Kristin, what's going on?" she asked.

"I needed to make you understand," I said, stepping inside, feeling the cool air on my skin but standing tall. "I enjoy being naked. It's part of who I am. But what you did—forcing Landon and me into that situation—was about control and humiliation, not freedom."

Joy looked uncomfortable but didn't back down. "Kristin, we never meant to humiliate you. We thought it was all in good fun."

"Maybe you thought that," I shot back, "but it had real consequences. You turned something I love into a spectacle, and it cost me someone I cared about."

Joy glanced at Michelle and Lea, then back at me. "We didn't realize it would have that effect. But you have to see, Kristin, not everyone can handle the level of openness you thrive on."

"And that's fine," I replied, my tone softening slightly. "But you need to respect my boundaries and my choices. If you can't do that, then we have a problem."

Joy nodded slowly. "I understand, Kristin. I'm sorry if we crossed a line. We'll try to be more mindful in the future."

I sighed, feeling a bit of the tension leave my shoulders. "Thank you. That's all I ask. Now, if you'll excuse me, I think I'll head back to my garden."

As I turned to leave, still naked and unashamed, I felt a small sense of victory. It wasn't just about winning an argument; it was about standing up for who I am and what I believe in while I was nude. I walked away from Joy's house with my head held high, knowing that while I may have lost Landon, I hadn't lost myself.

And that, in the end, was what mattered most.

Beyond the Garden

Gardening naked is a delight, but let's be honest—there's more to life than weeding in the buff and watering tomatoes with the breeze tickling your nether regions. Life beyond the garden offers endless opportunities for those who love the freedom of being naked and aren't afraid to embrace it. So, grab your metaphorical hat and sunscreen (because let's face it, you're not wearing anything else), and let's explore the hilariously liberating adventures that await us beyond the garden gate.

First up, there's the beach. Ah, the joy of a good nude beach! There's nothing quite like the feeling of sand between your toes and, well, everywhere else. I remember my first time at a nude beach. I walked onto the sand, towel in hand, feeling a bit like a nervous rabbit. But within minutes, the apprehension melted away, and I was frolicking in the waves like a carefree seal. There's a special kind of camaraderie at a nude beach—everyone's relaxed, unpretentious, and more than happy to share sunscreen (just be sure you're clear on where you need it applied!).

Then there's hiking. Nude hiking, or "free hiking," as the enthusiasts call it, is an exhilarating way to connect with nature. Imagine trekking through a forest, the dappled sunlight filtering through the trees, a gentle breeze on your skin, and not a care in the world. Of course, there's the occasional surprise meeting with a clothed hiker, which can be a bit awkward. I've perfected my casual wave and, "Beautiful day for a hike, isn't it?" Trust me, it breaks the ice faster than you can say "trail mix."

Speaking of activities, let's not forget yoga. Naked yoga is a trend that's been gaining traction, and for good reason. There's something profoundly freeing about practicing yoga without the constraint of clothing. You can stretch deeper, breathe easier, and fully connect with your body. Plus, it's a great way to embrace body positivity. Just remember to bring your own mat—I've learned the hard way that sharing yoga mats in a naked class is a no-no.

Public speaking might not be the first thing that comes to mind, but hear me out. I once attended a nudist convention where I had to give a talk about the joys of naked gardening. Standing in front of a crowd, baring it all—literally—was one of the most nerve-wracking yet empowering experiences of my life. If you can confidently discuss composting while in your birthday suit, you can tackle anything.

Traveling offers another set of adventures. There are nudist resorts and campsites all over the world, each offering a unique experience. Whether it's lounging by a pool in the south of France or exploring the rugged beauty of a naturist park in the Rockies, the sense of community and freedom is universal. Just remember to pack light—really light.

Social gatherings take on a whole new meaning when clothes are optional. Imagine a dinner party where the dress code is "come as you are." I once hosted a naked potluck, and let me tell you, it was an evening of laughter, incredible food, and some very interesting conversations. There's something about the lack of clothing that strips away pretense and brings people closer together. Just be careful when handling hot dishes—you don't want any accidents.

And let's not forget about the creative arts. Painting, sculpting, or even crafting while nude can be incredibly liberating. I took up body painting and discovered that the human body is a wonderful canvas. Plus, it's a fun way to spend an afternoon with friends—just make sure the paint is non-toxic and washable!

Of course, there are practical aspects to consider when living a nudist lifestyle beyond the garden. Always keep a wrap or towel handy for those unexpected moments when the doorbell rings or a delivery arrives. And it's wise to know the local laws and customs—what's acceptable at a nudist resort might not fly at your local grocery store.

Turning the Tables on Joy

Let me tell you about a day that still brings a smile to my face every time I think about it. It was a warm, sunny afternoon, perfect for some leisurely gardening. I was just finishing up my morning routine and decided to take a stroll around the neighborhood to admire everyone else's gardens. As I approached Joy's house, something caught my eye. There, in the middle of her yard, was Joy—completely naked, tending to her flower beds.

I had to blink a few times to make sure I wasn't seeing things. Joy, who had always been a bit judgmental about my love for naked gardening, was out there in all her natural glory! She looked serene and focused, clearly enjoying the experience. I couldn't help but chuckle at the irony of it all.

But then, the tables turned. Joy looked up and saw me standing there. Her eyes went wide, and she let out a squeak. She grabbed a towel from a nearby chair and wrapped it around herself, looking like a deer caught in headlights.

"Kristin! What are you doing here?" she stammered, her face turning as red as her roses.

I couldn't resist. With a mischievous grin, I pulled out my phone and snapped a quick photo. "I just wanted to take a walk and appreciate the gardens. But look what I found—Joy, the nudist gardener!"

Joy's jaw dropped. "Kristin, delete that photo right now!"

I laughed, waving my phone in the air. "Oh, no, Joy. I think I'll keep this one. Consider it payback for the time you took that photo of me and Landon."

She looked mortified, clutching the towel tighter. "That was different! We were just having fun!"

"And so am I," I replied, still grinning. "Isn't it funny how things come full circle?"

Joy sighed, realizing she was caught. "Alright, alright. You turned the tables on me. I get it."

I walked closer, lowering my phone. "So, Joy, what made you decide to try naked gardening?"

She hesitated, then shrugged. "I guess I wanted to see what all the fuss was about. And, well, I can see why you like it. It's... liberating."

I smiled, feeling a bit of the tension ease between us. "It is, isn't it? No hard feelings, Joy. I won't share the photo. But now you understand why it means so much to me."

Joy nodded, finally relaxing. "I do, Kristin. And I'm sorry for being so hard on you before. It's actually kind of amazing."

We stood there for a moment, two neighbors who had finally found common ground—in the most unexpected way. I handed her phone back, and she laughed, shaking her head.

"You really got me," she admitted.

I winked. "Consider it even. Now, how about we both get back to our gardens and enjoy this beautiful day?"

Joy smiled, dropping the towel and standing confidently. "Sounds like a plan."

Conclusion

And so, dear reader, we've come to the end of our delightful journey through the liberating and joyful world of naked gardening. From the practical tips and seasonal strategies to the hilarious and heartfelt stories of personal experiences, I hope this book has inspired you to shed more than just your gardening gloves and embrace the beauty and freedom of gardening in the nude.

Naked gardening is more than just a quirky hobby; it's a way of life that reconnects us with nature and with ourselves. It's about feeling the earth beneath our feet, the sun on our skin, and the breeze where the sun usually doesn't shine. It's about the simple pleasures of digging in the dirt, planting seeds, and watching them grow—all while celebrating the natural state of our bodies.

Throughout this book, we've explored the numerous benefits of naked gardening for both body and soul. We've learned how to prepare our gardens for each season, how to select the perfect plants, and how to maintain our gardens without losing our modesty—because, let's face it, we never had any to begin with!

We've shared laughs, shed tears, and maybe even a few clothes along the way. From confrontations with curious neighbors to the unexpected joys of community, naked gardening has proven to be an adventure filled with growth, connection, and a fair share of humorous mishaps.

But beyond the garden, this journey is about embracing who we are, unapologetically and confidently. It's about challenging societal norms, fostering body positivity, and finding peace and happiness in the simplest of activities. Naked gardening teaches us to be present, to appreciate the beauty of nature, and to celebrate our bodies in all their natural glory.

So, as you close this book and step into your garden, I encourage you to strip away your insecurities and embrace the freedom of naked gardening. Let the sun kiss your skin, the soil ground you, and the plants teach you about patience and growth. Whether you're a seasoned nudist or a curious beginner, may your gardening adventures be filled with laughter, love, and a deep connection to the natural world.

Thank you for joining me on this journey. Now, go forth and garden naked, my friends. The world is your garden, and it's time to let your true self bloom.

Happy naked gardening!

My New Bond with Joy

As the weeks passed, the bond between Joy and me grew stronger, nurtured by our shared love of naked gardening. The initial awkwardness had melted away, replaced by a sense of camaraderie and mutual respect. Joy's transformation from skeptical neighbor to enthusiastic nudist gardener was a delightful surprise, and it brought a new dynamic to our gardening routines.

One sunny Saturday morning, I was out in the garden, trimming the tomato plants and humming a cheerful tune. The gate creaked open, and Joy strolled in, a basket in one hand and a beaming smile on her face.

"Good morning, Kristin!" she called out. "Ready for another beautiful day in the garden?"

I waved her over, laughing. "Always! What's in the basket?"

She held it up proudly. "Freshly baked muffins. I thought we could use a snack break today."

We settled into our usual rhythm, tending to our plants side by side. There was something wonderfully liberating about working together in our natural state, without the barriers of clothing or pretense. The garden had become a sanctuary where we could be our true selves, and our friendship had flourished alongside the plants.

As we worked, we chatted about everything under the sun—our favorite gardening tips, our plans for the upcoming season, and even a bit of harmless neighborhood gossip. Joy had become not just a gardening buddy, but a true friend.

"Remember when you first saw me gardening naked?" I teased, grinning at her.

Joy laughed, shaking her head. "How could I forget? I thought I'd seen it all until that moment. Now look at us!"

"It's amazing how things change," I said, pausing to wipe the sweat from my forehead. "I never thought we'd be here, doing this together."

Joy nodded, a thoughtful look in her eyes. "You know, Kristin, I'm grateful for that day. It pushed me out of my comfort zone and into something wonderful. Naked gardening has changed me—made me more confident, more connected to nature."

I smiled, feeling a warm glow of pride. "I'm glad, Joy. It's done the same for me. And it's been even better sharing it with a friend."

We continued working in comfortable silence for a while, the only sounds being the rustle of leaves and the chirping of birds. At one point, Joy looked over at me, a mischievous twinkle in her eye.

"Want to race to see who can harvest the most carrots?" she challenged.

I laughed, setting down my tools. "You're on!"

We dashed to the carrot patch, laughing and competing with the playful energy of children. By the time we finished, we were both breathless and covered in dirt, but it didn't matter. The joy of the moment was worth every smudge.

As the sun began to set, casting a golden glow over the garden, we sat down on a bench, enjoying the muffins Joy had brought. The sense of accomplishment and contentment was palpable.

"Today was perfect," Joy said, her voice soft with happiness.

"It really was," I agreed. "And I wouldn't have it any other way."

Joy and I continued to garden together regularly, our friendship deepening with each passing day. The garden became our haven, a place where we could escape the stresses of daily life and find peace in the simple act of nurturing plants.

In the end, naked gardening wasn't just about being free from clothes—it was about being free to be ourselves, to embrace life with all its messiness and beauty. And as Joy and I tended to our little corner of the world, we discovered that the most important thing we were growing was our friendship.

So, if you ever find yourself in our neighborhood on a sunny day, don't be surprised to see two naked ladies laughing, working, and enjoying the garden together. Because sometimes, the best things in life happen when you're willing to bare it all and share it with a friend.

<u>Gardening Naked</u>

In the dawn's early light, when the world is still,
I step to my garden, over dewy grass and hill.
No cloth to bind me, no shoes to tread,
Barefoot and bare-skinned, to the earth I'm wed.

The sun kisses my skin, a gentle, warm embrace,
As I tend to my plants in this sacred, private space.
The soil, cool and soft, beneath my naked toes,
A tactile reminder of the life that grows.

With hands ungloved, I dig and I sow,
Feeling every grain, every root below.
The breeze whispers secrets, rustling the leaves,
As I move through my garden, my spirit believes.

In the rhythm of nature, I find my pace,
In this unclothed freedom, I find my place.
Each flower I nurture, each vegetable I tend,
In the raw, pure moment, I find a friend.

No need for pretense, no need for disguise,
Just me and the earth, beneath open skies.
The birds serenade me, the bees hum along,
In this naked dance, I am nature's song.

Through seasons of change, from summer to spring,
In the heart of my garden, I find everything.
The cycles of life, so simple, so grand,
All understood better with bare feet in the sand.

So here's to the freedom, to the joy I've embraced,
In the garden of life, where nothing's misplaced.
Naked and natural, pure and unplanned,
In the heart of my garden, my soul understands.

For in the act of gardening, stripped to the core,
I've found more than produce, I've found something more.
A connection to earth, to self, to sky,
In the garden, naked, I truly fly.

Printed in Great Britain
by Amazon